A PROTEST

ADDRESSED TO THE

HON. SECRETARY OF THE INTERIOR,

—BY—

LOUIS JANIN, ESQ.,

OF THE

NEW ORLEANS AND WASHINGTON BAR,

AGAINST THE

HON. WILLIS DRUMMOND,

COMMISSIONER OF THE GENERAL LAND OFFICE,

AND THE

Maladministration of the United States Land Office at New Orleans.

NEW ORLEANS:
A. W. HYATT. STATIONER AND PRINTER 38 CAMP STREET,
1873.

NEW ORLEANS, October 18TH, 1873

HON. COLUMBUS DELANO,

Secretary of the Interior:

SIR—The contemptuous disfavor with which the Commissioner of the General Land Office treats land matters coming before him from Louisiana, the offensive discourtesy with which he treats me, the oldest man and oldest lawyer practicing before him, and endeavors to injure my law firm and those citizens of Louisiana who have confidence in us, compel me to address you, his superior, for redress.

An unpleasant incident which gave rise to the present difficulty is explained in a letter which I addressed to the Commissioner, under date of the 10th inst., of which I enclose two printed copies. At the foot of this present letter I shall annex an affidavit verifying the contents of that letter.

This morning I received from Mr. E. H. Foster, the Surveyor General of the United States in Louisiana, the following letter:

"SURVEYOR GENERAL'S OFFICE,

"New Orleans, La., October 17th, 1873.

"MR. LOUIS JANIN,

"Bourbon St., New Orleans:

"*Sir*—The following is a copy of a telegram received yesterday from the Commissioner of the General Land Office:

" 'WASHINGTON, D. C., October 16, 1873.

" 'U. S. SURVEYOR GENL.,

" 'N. O. La.:

" 'Until further orders, deny the firm of Louis Janin & Son access to your records and papers, unless for the purpose of preparing charges against Government officials, and refuse to recognize them as attorneys before your office under any circumstances.

" 'WILLIS DRUMMOND,

" '*Commissioner.*'

"Of course the authority of the Commissioner to give these directions, above copied, is unquestioned.

"Very respectfully,

"E. W. FOSTER,

"*Surveyor General.*"

I am thus impelled to the disagreeable task of denouncing persons against whom, except Julian Neville, I have no private grievances. And I shall prefer charges that will fill you with astonishment. But as it is apparent from the telegrams of Commissioner Drummond, and the tone of his letter to my firm of the 2d inst., that I cannot expect from him even a courteous hearing and considerate attention, I shall submit my charges and proofs to you.

For some time past I have been confined to my rooms by an accident, which even now prevents me from walking. I expect, however, in a few days to be well enough to be able to visit offices whence my evidence is to come. As, however, I have a great deal of professional business to occupy me, I shall not bestow much time for the present on these charges, but certainly enough to show *that Sulakowski's and Ross' survey of T. 12 S. R. 11 E. S.* E. District of Louisiana is grossly incorrect, calculated to work great confusion and mischief, ought never to have been approved, and should be rejected in toto as worse than worthless.

I have the honor to be, sir,

Very respectfully,

Your obedient servant,

LOUIS JANIN.

Louis Janin, being duly sworn, deposes and says, that the contents of this letter, and of his above mentioned letter to the Hon. Willis Drummond of the 10th inst., as stated from his own information, are true, and as stated upon information derived from others, he believes them to be true.

LOUIS JANIN.

Subscribed and sworn to before the undersigned.

JULES MOSSY,

U. S. Commissioner.

NEW ORLEANS, October 22d, 1873.

HON. COLUMBUS DELANO,

Secretary of the Interior:

SIR—Please notice that the letter I addressed to you under date of the 18th inst. is verified by my oath. So, also, will be this letter.

You will recollect the decision you made on the 5th of January, 1871, upon the fraudulent pretensions of Mrs. Myra Clark Gaines, under claim No. 104, confirmed in the name of Daniel Clark. The frauds which it is now attemped to accomplish under color of Sulakowski's and Ross' survey, approved by the Surveyor General, are as glaring as that in which your decision defeated Mrs. Gaines.

It is generally believed that a number of persons enjoying particular favor are interested in the partition of the spoils. I have neither the disposition nor the time at present to trace these frauds to their intended beneficiaries, but if there is any foundation for the common rumor and general belief, I have no doubt that the United States Receiver, Mr. Julian Neville, will be found to have been selected as an associate for the purpose of preventing my interference and exposure of the fraud in the Land Office. The aim of these persons is to speculate at the expense of the holders of old land titles. They know that I am the only surviving lawyer much acquainted with the titles near this city. Indeed, it is well known that I have had more professional employment in suits involving these titles than any lawyer in Louisiana. Messrs. Lott and Neville, the Register and Receiver, have had the skill of gaining over to their side Mr. Commissioner Drummond, from whom I received this morning a most offensive letter, dated the 15th inst. The Commissioner, a copy of whose letter I enclose, treats me as a criminal for venturing to question the integrity and capacity of his subordinates. But all that, however unpleasant, will not deter me from performing the part of a good citizen, for which task I consider myself fitted by my long experience, and because I have no political aspirations or political antipathies. I shall prove my case like a well prepared law-suit, by unquestionable evidence. For the first time since several weeks I am now able to leave my residence to procure plans and copies of writings for my case. I shall prove that Sulakowski's and Ross' survey of T. 12 S., R. 11 and 12 E., S. E. District of Louisiana, *approved by Surveyor General E. W. Foster,* can never be the basis of official action by the Land Department of the Government, and must be entirely set aside; that it is so grossly erroneous that it would give rise to numerous law-suits if it were treated as presumptive evidence of the location and condition of claims and titles that have remained undisturbed for a century.

The first wrong was the kind of contract the Surveyor General made. Mr. Gascon, the Surveyor General's chief clerk, told me only yesterday that the price paid for this survey was only $8000. I shall produce the testimony of one of the only two surviving surveyors who have had much to do with these localities and the titles of these lands, showing that on account of the numerous conflicts, the very indefinite and loose manner in which grants were made by the colonial governments, and the destruction of the most important evidence, such a survey, properly made, would be worth fully $50,000, and could not be finished under a number of years. Mr. Wm. J. McCulloh, who was for many years Surveyor General of the United States for the State of Louisiana, and a most efficient and able public officer, states to me that on one occasion, when he was Surveyor General, he was authorized to offer $50 a mile for the survey of this township, but could get no competent surveyor to accept it, and would not himself have undertaking it for $150 a mile. Mr. Foster, however, gave out the contract for much less, but how? He found an impoverished surveyor in the Parish of Terrebonne, who, owing to the general stagnation and depression of business, had nothing to do, and was glad to undertake anything that promised him a temporary living, whether he could do the work or not. The name of this surveyor was Sulakowski, and he was forced to divide his pitiable fee with Mr. Foster's brother-in-law, one Ross, who is a carpenter by trade, and not a surveyor, and who was to advance to Sulakowski the necessary money. Sulakowski had not the least idea of the difficulty of the work.

If he had possessed the requisite knowledge, he could not honestly have undertaken it for such a price and within the time allowed for it. The money he received would not have kept him a live during half the time the work would have required to be honestly done. The General Land Office would not, we hope, have ordered the Register and Receiver to notify claimants to file and sustain, before the 1st of next December, their opposition to the entries *by Dr. A. W. Smythe* of lands reported by the Surveyor General as swamp lands, and almost immediately afterwards sold by the Register of the State Land Office *to Dr. Smythe, as lands subject to tidal overflow, for twenty-five cents per acre,* if it, that is, the General Land Office, had possessed the least information concerning the condition of the records of the land office and of the public depositories of deeds in this city. Besides, the act of Congress of June 10th, 1872, gives to claimants three years from its date within which to file their claims.

Perfect strangers to this locality, like Ross and Sulakowski, could not possibly have executed that survey properly; they would have been deficient in the necessary knowledge of the points of departure.

A very erroneous impression has prevailed in the General Land Office and its subordinate offices, to-wit: that any land in Louisiana, the title to which had not been expressly confirmed, was public land. Complete grants which separated the land from the royal domain under the Colonial Government, are valid without confirmation. (See the letter of Albert Gallatin, Secretary of the Treasury, of March 30th, 1805, Vol. I of Laws, Opinions and Instructions concerning Public Lands, p. 666, and numerous other authorities on this subject collected in my points, and in the decision of the Supreme Court of Louisiana, in the case of Lavergne's heirs vs. Elkins' heirs, 17 La. Rep., p. 220.) On Sulakowski's and Ross' map, nearly the whole lower part of the City of New Orleans is represented "no confirmation found." When I forward to you the evidence in support of this sworn statement, it will be proved to you that the whole of this land is covered by French concessions. All French concessions I have ever seen were complete grants. It will appear from the decision of the Court in the case of Lavergne's heirs, above referred to, that there was then in the United States Land Office at New Orleans, a very large folio volume, containing the records of French and Spanish grants. As was stated by the Supreme Court of Louisiana, extracts from this book were always considered legal evidence of the grants. There were in that land office other volumes of complete and others of inchoate grants; and extracts from these volumes were also always considered as evidence in the courts. Most of these records and the other contents of that land office were destroyed by fire in 1865, but of the oldest and largest a great many grants were preserved and are still in the land office in a perfectly legible condition. These records were the "public records in which grants of land, warrants or orders of survey, or any other evidence of claims to land, derived from either the French or Spanish Governments, may have been recorded," mentioned in the 5th section of the act of Congress, of March 2d, 1805, creating the first Board of Commissioners for ascertaining and adjusting the titles and claims to land within the territory of Orleans and the District of Louisiana. The old inhabitants of these regions, and particularly the owners of land in the vicinity of New Orleans, would not have there present troubles about their titles, if this Board of Commissioners had done its duty as defined by that same act and section, which was "to decide in a summary way, according to justice and equity, on all claims filed with the Register or Recorder, in conformity with the provisions of this act, and *on all complete French or Spanish grants, the evidence of which, though not thus filed*, may be found of record on the public records of such grants; which decision shall be laid before Congress in the manner hereinafter directed, and be subject to their determination thereon."

I believe that this was not done in a single instance. But I submit that a surveyor who is under contract for a survey of a township, is bound to make inquiry about at least the *complete grants* described in the above mentioned section of the act of Congress of March 2, 1805.

I am confident that neither Sulakowski nor the Surveyor General ever examined the remains of the original records still extant in the land office. But I did so some weeks ago, and found there the two complete French grants which cover the ground which was *purchased by Dr. Smythe as land subject to tidal overflow, at twenty-five cents per acre*, both grants being made to the same person and for the same lands, varying only very little. One of these grants is as legible as when it was written; the greater part of the other is also still legible. To show with what degree of carelessness this survey and plan were made, I beg leave to relate a remarkable incident, of which my knowledge and recollection are perfect.

Some two years ago I visited the office of the Surveyor General here, and there saw Sulakowski at work on that map. He had heard that I had had many suits about lands lying within the boundaries of said map. He asked me whether I knew any title to a large piece of ground which, on his map, is now described as section 119, and as the claim confirmed to J. Bte. Castillon, O. B., 308. 9th claim. I referred him to my old suit of Pontalba, et al vs. Copeland, et als., 3 La. Annual Rep.. p. 86, the record of which is still in the office of the Clerk of the Supreme Court of Louisiana. In that record he would have found copies of the two grants to LeBreton whence the title of the Canal Bank to the land entered by *Dr. Smythe* is derived. Sulakowski then laid the Castillon claim down as it now appears on the map. On a subsequent occasion I saw on this map that he had written on an adjoining tract, section 137, "John Arrowsmith, under the Mauleon grant, 137.60 acres." I told Sulakowski that this land was a part of the claim of Jean Bte. Macarty, of December 22, 1795, which, although confirmed, was defeated in the suit of Pontalba et al vs. Copeland et als., by an anterior grant and confirmation. The Mauleon grant is the claim confirmed in the name of Castillon, and which I represented in the case of Pontalba vs. Copeland. Half of it belonged to the Chalon family, and Sulakowski, who thought that he had made the discovery that the Mauleon grant extended over the triangle bearing Arrowsmith's name, (which it does not), went to see Mr. J. O. Chalon, offering to give him information showing that his family were entitled to more land than they had recovered, lying within the boundaries of his surveying contract, provided they pay him for it. Mr. Chalon excused himself by saying that his family had no money to spare, and were content to rely upon me as their counsel. This resembles a similar attempt of Julian Neville to make money out of the information to be found in his office, and which will be brought to your notice.

The triangle above mentioned is moreover covered by the patent to General Lafayette, with which I am very familiar, because I recovered under it Sulakowski's section 85, bearing the name of the heirs of General Lafayette. But when, subsequently, other counsel brought suit for the heirs of Lafayette, for the purpose of claiming the land behind the tract I had recovered, and as far back as the piece marked with Arrowsmith's name, the parties interested in those lands, made a compromise with the holders of the Macarty claim, and I defeated the claims of the heirs of Lafayette to this tract with the Macarty title mainly, because the latter had been confirmed before the issuance of the Lafayette patent.

This is a fair specimen of the history of titles about New Orleans. Nearly all of these titles have undergone judicial investigation. It would be criminal to allow such settlements to be disturbed by an ignorant surveyor. Sulakowsky became gradually aware of the difficulty of getting accurate information, and, in his despair, said that as he could not get it he would go on as well as he could without that information. I have shown how he disregarded the information I gave him. He did the work at hap hazard, and having fallen out with the carpenter Ross, his associate, and being very necessitous, he finished the work as quickly as possible.

The survey is full of the grossest errors, of which conclusive proof will be furnished you. I shall not here specify these errors, but the most satisfactory evidence of them will soon be submitted by me. You will, of course, readily believe that, being under oath and very familiar with the subject, I do not advance this lightly. I have no doubt that it can be proved, whenever inquiry is made, that Mr. Foster is interested in speculations incompatible with his official duties, in conjunction with his brother, brother-in-law and other relations. Of one fact the Department has already been apprised by Mr. Jas. L. Bradford, a lawyer of this city, whom, however, I have not seen for upwards of a year. This is substantially his charge: When secession took place in Louisiana, there had been received in the Surveyor General's office, but not yet approved, some one or more township surveys, executed under contracts. After secession, several other such surveys were returned into the office of the Confederate Land Commissioner. All the papers of that office were surrendered at Shreveport to General Herron, now Recorder of Mortgages in this city, and went into the hands of Mr. E. W. Foster, United States Surveyor General. These maps bear on their face the word "Null." Mr. Foster afterwards contracted with a Mr. Robinson, and probably with other friends and relations, for the re-survey of these townships, and those re-surveys were approved and paid for, as if the land had been actually resurveyed. But that was not the case. When these pretended re-surveys are compared with the maps that came from the Confederate Commissioner, it will be found that they are copies, *literatim et verbatim*, of the plans in the Confederate Commissioner's office, corresponding in every particular, in area, length and direction of lines, etc., with the plans from which they were evidently copied. Such a coincidence between two surveys of a township, made by different surveyors, is perfectly impossible, except upon the pypothesis that the one was copied from the other.

It would require too much space for me to notice here at any length the case of Julian Neville, which is less important than that of Mr. Foster. But we can prove that he has openly avowed his determination to disregard the laws regulating his official fees; that while his salary is but a small one, he has declared that he would make his office worth $5000 a year; that he has exacted fees for copies which never were heard of before; that he has solicited bribes, and that he and the Register have treated most offensively persons who, like Mr. S. Z. Relf and myself, will not submit to their exactions. I am certain that these things and much more can be proved by gentlemen who are unwilling to volunteer their testimony for fear of incurring the coarse vituperation of Julian Neville, but who will give their testimony if called upon officially to do so. If you could direct officially some gentleman, such as the United States District Attorney, to swear and examine the witnesses whom we would bring before him, with liberty to us to examine them also after giving notice to persons against whom their testimony will be directed, the Department would soon be in possession of proper evidence concerning the character of its officials here, and probably also ascertain whether they are not chargeable with illegal practices, and whether they, and how many of them are interested, together with other United States and State officials, in the principal fraud which we are employed to resist. If such an investigation can be entered into, I would request that it be done promptly, as my professional engagements will soon compel me to return to Washington. Such an investigation, if confided to proper hands, would be hailed as a token of returning justice to this population.

In my letter to you of the 18th inst., *I called the entries made by Dr. Smythe an unblushing fraud. This Dr. Smythe, who is the physician of the Charity Hospital here, is evidently only an interposed person.* Mr. Foster, the Surveyor General, declared the lands in question to be swamp and overflowed lands, which should be listed to the State, and a very short time afterwards Mr. John Ray, the Register of the State Land Office, sold them to Dr. Smythe, as lands subject to tidal overflow, at twenty-five cents per acre. These lands are held by the Canal Bank and its assigns under a complete grant of October 6, 1857, which Sulakowski overlooked, because he did not examine with sufficient attention the record of the case of Pontalba vs. Copeland, 3 Annual, Rep., 86, in which it is copied, nor the remains of the old book of French grants, of which many old grants, and among them the greater part of this one, still exist. But what can be more absurd than to represent as swamp and subject to tidal overflow, a navigable canal through which a great proportion of the building materials, brick, lumber, wood, etc., which are used here are brought to this city, and which was laid out in 1832 by General, then Lieutenant Delafield; and the fine shell road along the canal; the hotels and pleasure grounds at the end of the canal on the Lake shore; another public house with a garden, called the Half Way House; a toll gate and the toll-collector's house; a tract of land formerly used as a race course and now sold for a cemetery; the Oakland Riding Park, a place of great resort for pic-nics and other public amusements—in short, lands on which several hundred people permanently reside, and part of which is the highest land in the vicinity of New Orleans, and never was overflowed by breaks or crevasses of the levees on the river, or by backwater from the lakes, and not even during the terrific hurricanes of 1812 and 1831.

All this land covered *by Dr. Smythe's purchase*, is within the incorporated limits of the Cities of New Orleans and Carrollton. More than that, these lands lie within the draining works of New Orleans, intended to improve the salubrity of the City, for which every inch of ground in the city, high or low, is taxed, on which nearly ten millions of dollars have been expended, and which are now progressing at an expense to the city of about thirty thousand dollars a month, and part of which is protected on its upper side, and a portion of its front by the most substantial levees of the State, and crossed by the New Orleans, Jackson and Great Northern Railroad. All this was ignored by Sulakowski and Foster. Nor was it represented on Sulakowski's map as claimed by anybody. I have not seen Sulakowski's field notes, but Mr. Foster declared this land to be swamp land and subject to overflow, and Mr. John Ray, the Register of the State Land Office, sold it to Dr. A. W. Smythe—all of them knowing perfectly well the real character of the land. Was it possible for any one acquainted with these localities not to suspect glaring and unblushing fraud in these transactions, even without the aid of what has since leaked out? This will be still more apparent when the State legislation on this subject is considered. A law of March 17, 1859, (acts 1859, p. 159), first permitted land subject to tidal overflow and listed to the State, to be sold at twenty-five cents per acre. This law was reproduced in the Revised Statutes of 1870, compiled by John Ray, as section 2793. It was re-enacted, with interesting modifications, by the 3d section of an act of the Legislature of Louisiana, of May 31, 1871, the 13th section of which repeals all laws inconsistent with it. The first two laws relative to such lands, passed in 1859 and 1870 required that lands intended to be sold as lands subject to tidal overflow should first be patented to the State, and that the sales should be made by the Register and State Treasurer, who was ex officio Treasurer of the Land Office. The amended act of May 31, 1871, omits the word patented, and authorizes the Register alone to sell. By that law John Ray was enabled to make the sale to *Dr. Smythe*. Was that law passed for that express purpose? Who can doubt it?

Mr. Julian Neville's insolent letter to me of the 17th of last month occasioned the difficulty here spoken of. I wrote to my sons and partners in Washington what I saw was going on here, without, however, asking for any action by the Department upon the matter, and at the same time, on the 18th ult., wrote a very courteous letter to Commissioner Drummond. enclosing a copy and the original of Julian Neville's letter, and explaining that I had withdrawn the papers with the consent of the Register for the purpose of examining them and having them translated. I further stated that having received such an insolent letter from the Register and Receiver, I could no longer hold intercourse with those persons, and that, therefore, I would avail myself of the right given to claimants by the act of Congress of June 22, 1860, and June 10, 1872, to file their claims and prosecute them in the United States District Court, and that consequently I would not return the papers I had obtained from the Land Office, but would file them with the petition in said District Court, where they now are.

I beg leave to enclose that very letter, which is correct in every particular, except in the statement that the papers I had received had been *filed* by Mr. Finney. In point of fact, they do not bear the least mark showing them to have been filed in that office, though they were copied there. That letter was read by my son, Albert C. Janin, to Commissioner Drummond, who abruptly exclaimed: "I won't listen to anything until the papers are returned," and could only be induced to pay any attention to what my son was reading by the evident determination of the latter to insist upon his hearing my statement of the matter.

Then my son communicated to the Commissioner the suspicions of fraud I had thrown out in my private correspondence with them, and this produced the Commissioner's extraordinary letter to my firm of the 2d instant, (a copy of which I enclose), in which we are treated as impertinent intruders into the business of the Department, soundly rated for daring to suspect the integrity of the officials the Land Department has in this State, and defied to prefer charges under oath and supported by evidence. This letter was replied to by my son Albert C. Janin, under date of the 4th instant.

It is not agreeable to me to undertake the exposure of every fraud that comes to my knowledge; but the truly threatening tone of the Commissioner's letter of the 2d of this month compelled me to repel the imputation of being afraid to speak out, and I therefore wrote to him the letter under date of the 10th instant, which I afterwards had printed, and of which I took the liberty of sending you two copies.

Commissioner Drummond has thus forced me to perform the part of a detective. I have, therefore, taken the trouble to make this long statement under oath. I hope it may lead to an investigation, and, to use the Commissioner's own language in his letter of the 2d instant., "place the Government in a position to rid itself of corrupt and dishonest officials." I will take the further trouble of producing the necessary evidence, if you will permit me to prosecute the matter before any officer of your Department other than the one whose personal hostility to me is so apparent that I could expect from him neither courtesy nor justice.

Under date of the 15th instant he addressed to my firm a letter of which the following is the closing part:

"In view of your continued refusal ro return the records borrowed, as aforesaid, of the local Land Office at New Orleans, it becomes my duty, as an officer, to take such measures as may be necessary to protect the Government and parties having business before this office and subordinate offices from a further interference with public records by parties who have wantonly violated the confidence reposed in them and disregarded well established rules of professional propriety and practice, and I have, therefore, now to inform you that from and after this date, and until further notice from the Commissioner of this office, you will not be permitted to examine any record or paper filed herein, unless such examination be for the purpose of obtaining data in support of any charges you may desire to make against officers of the Government, nor from this date, until such notice, will you be recognized as attorneys in any case now pending or which may hereafter be presented to the General Land Office.

"Very respectfully,

"WILLIS DRUMMOND,

"*Commissioner.*"

Commissioner Drummond thus unkertakes to disbar me and my sons and to destroy our land business, which, as he well knows, is very large. He harbors an undisguised animosity towards me, because I defend the rights of my clients with zeal and pertinacity. You may recollect, Mr. Secretary, that I twice called upon you for the purpose of inducing you to change the form of the scrip which has to be issued to successful claimants under the act of June 22, 1860, and which the Commissioner refuses to make assignable or transferable by delivery—a question in which the Cities of New Orleans and Baltimore, the Hon. Caleb Cushing, and other clients of mine are interested. On one occasion I was accompanied by the Hon. Postmaster General, and on the other by Hon. L. A Sheldon, who the former as a citizen of Maryland and the latter as a representative from Louisiana feel an interest in the fine legacy which the late John McDonogh left to the two cities of large land claims, upon which I have obtained judgments. These cities cannot locate wild lands with their scrip; they must be enabled to sell it; but the form in which the Commissioner issues it depreciates its value, and renders a sale of it very difficult. Not one sensible reason have I ever heard for refusing to make the scrip assignable. It does not make the least difference to the Government, and I truly believe the Commissioner refused it because I proposed it, and perhaps also because it might have benefited Louisiana people, for whose rights I am convinced he has a great contempt. You will, perhaps, remember that you called Mr. Drummond before you in my presence, and that he was considerably nettled by my showing, in answer to his objection that he must follow precedent, that not a single acre of scrip had ever been issued under the act of 1860, and that consequently no precedent existed.

Commissioner Drummond undertakes to disbar me upon a simple unsupported statement of Julian Neville, without taking into consideration my statement or investigating the matter. This is certainly the most extraordinary proceeding ever attempted by a public officer holding a quasi-judicial appointment. Mr. Drummond cannot point to a single discourteous word in the very extensive correspondence I have had with his office since his appointment. But being now personally attacked and insulted by him, I shall not mince the matter, but shall review his course towards me and my sons in the language expressive of my true feelings.

If Mr. Drummond belongs to the legal profession, he must know that the bar is a representative body, maintaining the rights of its members and its clients. One of the duties of that body is, not to allow itself to be cowed by offensive and prejudiced judges, but to resist them and to appeal from them to public opinion. If the Commissioner had intended to be just and fair towards me, he would have judged of my character, not by the statements of Julian Neville, but by seeking information from purer sources. He might have ascertained that I am one of the oldest members of the bar of the Supreme Court of the United States, having been admitted in the January term of 1846 (4 Howard, 503), and he would have addressed himself, for information as to my professional standing, to the Judges of the Supreme Court, the members of the Washington bar, or to his predecessors, Messrs. Jos. S. Wilson, J. M. Edmunds, John Wilson, Thos. A. Hendricks and James Shields.

But it is evident that Mr. Drummond knows as little of me as he does of Julian Neville and the latter's reputation here. He knows me only as a pertinacious defender of Louisiana land claims. He no doubt knows a great deal of railroad land grants, of which I know nothing; but I am certain he knows nothing, do doubt for want of opportunity, of Louisiana land claims, with which I have been occupied the greater part of a long life, and of which many persons consider me a good judge, among them the Judges of the former Supreme Courts and the older lawyers of Louisiana. And precisely because I believe that I possess accurate knowledge on the subject, I resist the encroachments of the ill-informed General Land Office upon what I consider sacred rights, and for which, to use the language of Chief Justice Marshall, in Foster and Elam vs. Neilson, 2 Pet., "the faith of the nation is pledged."

If Mr. Drummond is a member of my profession, I have to inform him that I am as much his senior in practice as I am in years, and I repel with indignation the charge of professional misconduct and breach of faith which he no doubt made in a moment of ill-advised ebullition of temper, such as he exhibited when my son, Albert C. Janin, read to him, despite all sorts of ill-natured interruptions, the first letter I wrote to him on this subject, under date of the 18th ultimo. I can assure him that this incident excites a good deal of attention here, and I have as yet not seen a single gentleman who does not approve my course after the reception of the insolent letter of the Register and Receiver of the 17th ultimo, and fully agree with me that no decent lawyer, North or South, would have acted differently.

The charges made by the Commissioner in his letter to my firm of the 15th instant, part of which I have copied into this letter, are coarse and offensive, particularly when preferred against a person so much his senior in practice and years, and who is apparently defenceless against him, except in extreme cases, when official annoyance assumes intolerable proportions and recourse to a higher authority becomes necessary. But these charges are not more coarse and offensive than they are absurd. I have proved this in my letter to the Commissioner of the 10th instant, which I have verified by my oath, and in the letter I sent to you on the 18th instant. But I will briefly recapitulate the matter.

By the act of June 22, 1860, claimants may, in certain cases, submit their claims either to the board composed of the Register and Receiver, or to the United States District Court. My friends, Messrs. Lea, Finney and Miller, the regular counsel of the Canal Bank, filed its claim for confirmation with the Register and Receiver, and deposited for recording with their notice of a claim a number of documents, being copies of the titles recorded in various offices, by which their property was conveyed from hand to hand from the year 1784 down. All of these papers, except one, were merely copies of documents contained in public offices, which anybody can have copied. This one document was an original report of a survey made by Carlos Trudeau, the royal surveyor under the Spanish Government. When I was afterwards employed in the case, at the instance of Messrs. Lea, Finney and Miller, I looked at these papers in the Land Office, and finding that they could not conveniently be examined there and required translation, I requested Mr. Lott to let me take them home for that purpose, which request he unhesitatingly granted. Mr. Lott is a young man of good manners and evidently of much more intelligence and better education than Julian Neville, and I know nothing against him except that he signed the insulting letters copied into my printed letter to Commissioner Drummond of the 10th instant, and the suspicious circumstance, which I have learned from a reliable source, that his two sureties are interested in the Smythe speculation. This, of course, I know only from hearsay.

The loan of such papers, under such circumstances, to the counsel of the party by whom they were presented as evidence, never was refused. By the act of June 22, 1860, the evidence had to be exhibited and recorded, but not to be retained. Accordingly these papers were deposited for recording in the office of the Register and Receiver, but not filed. They are now filed in the District Court of the United States in this city, they do not show the least indication of having been in the Land Office, and were, in fact, not filed there. The only proof that they ever were there is that they are recorded in that office.

The only use of such documents is to be examined and recorded, and that has already been done with them. They were never meant to be retained in the Land Office. It was never imagined by any one before Commissioner Drummond and the present Register and Receiver that the title papers of claimants should remain in that office. This is a most extraordinary and absurd proposition. Thousands of claims have been filed in the different United States Land Offices in Louisiana for confirmation, and in those of them which have not been destroyed by fire hardly any original titles can be found, except a few which have been left there by accident, death or negligence.

Who will believe that any act of Congress would require of parties, before their claims should be recognized, that they deposit their original titles in the Land Office, and thus relinquish the custody of them? If the people of this Land District had formerly done so, their titles would now have been destroyed by fire, as nearly the whole contents of the Land Office were in 1865.

But this case is much stronger, and the assumption of the Commissioner and the Register and Receiver, that our evidence should be left in the Land Office after it has been recorded, is most preposterous. It is quite contrary to the invariable practice of that office as dictated by common sense and not prohibited by law. Before the fire of 1865, that Land Office was filled with a large number of volumes containing copies of the evidence that had been submitted by claimants, and all of which, was possibly the exception of a few straggling and forgotten sheets, had been returned. Nobody ever before imagined that important original documents should be left in an office from which papers are frequently stolen. Besides, the papers I withheld in this case are not originals, with the single exception of a report, or, as it is here called a "process verbal" of survey, by Carlos Trudeau. Of all the others copies could be obtained by applying to the offices where the originals are deposited and bound up. Moreover, these identical documents are now *filed* in the United States District Court, and open to the inspection of everybody

The whole attack upon me by Julian Neville and Commissioner Drummond is most unwarranted and inexcusable. In Neville's case it is the result of disappointed greed for fees lost to him by my withdrawal of the case from his jurisdiction, and its probable consequences. For what lawyer having the least self respect will go before a board composed of such officials, when he has the right to take his case into a court of justice?

It required the ingenuity of Messrs. Drummond, Lott and Neville to question the right of a claimant to withdraw from the Land Office his own suit and to take along with him the evidence he had submitted, in order to file it in a court of justice. What possible use could the Land Office make of such evidence?

In Commissioner Drummond's case this attack is the result, not of a sense of official duty, but of personal hostility, such as, owing to human infirmity, sometimes arrises between a judge and a lawyer practising before him, but probably never was shown in a manner so undisguised and unwarranted. I have a better command over my temper than Mr. Drummond has, and I am sure that I have never, during my intercourse with him, given him the least ground for complaint against me, unless it be by refusing to accept his decisions and rulings as legal gospel, or by expressions contained in this letter, which his aggressiveness has extorted from me.

I therefore request, Mr. Secretary, in justice to my rights and to the honored profession of which you are a distinguished and I a very old member, that you will suggest to the Commissioner that he rescind the orders excluding me from the General Land Office at Washington and its subordinate offices in this city.

I say nothing here of the attempted exclusion of my sons and partners, for the Commissioner himself can hardly seriously suppose that he has the right to disbar persons who had no connection whatever with the transaction upon which he basis his orders, but were, in point of fact, hundreds of miles away from the scene of action.

I have the honor to be, sir, very respectfully,

Your obedient servant,

LOUIS JANIN.

Louis Janin, being duly sworn, deposes that the facts stated in the foregoing letter as of his own knowledge, are true, and the facts therein stated upon information derived from others, he believes to be true.

LOUIS JANIN.

Sworn to and subscribed before me.

JULES MOSSY,

U. S. Commissioner of La.

APPENDIX.

NEW ORLEANS, September 18TH, 1873.

HON. WILLIS DRUMMOND,

Commissioner of the General Land Office:

SIR—On the 16th of last July the New Orleans Canal Banking Company, a well known bank in this city, instituted proceedings in the New Orleans Land Office, claiming the confirmation of their title to a tract of land on which a canal leading from New Orleans to the Lake Pontchartrain, and a fine macademised shell road on the borders of the canal, have been constructed.

Messrs. Lea, Finney and Miller, the regular attorneys of the Canal Bank, filed the claim and a number of documents, being evidence in support of it. But, after pursuing the subject further and being unable to find the original title, they advised the Canal Bank to employ me in this and other land claims, telling the Bank that I was better acquainted with the land titles of this State and the language in which they are written.

It is but lately that I was employed in this case, and I found in the Land Office nineteen documents enumerated in a list which was filed by my friend Mr. Finney, of which I enclose a copy. These documents were mostly in French and Spanish, and had to be translated.

On the 8th instant I requested Mr. Lott to let me take these papers to my lodgings, that I might examine them, take notes of them, and have them translated. I could not conveniently employ more than one translator, and that was not his exclusive business, and notwithstanding his industry he could not finish the translations before yesterday afternoon. Yesterday evening I found on my table, to my great astonishment, a letter of which the following is a copy:

"U. S. CONSOLIDATED LAND OFFICE,

"New Orleans, La., Jan. 17th, 1873.

"LOUIS JANIN,

"Attorneys at Law,

"*No. 79 Bienville Street.*

"SIR—You obtained from this office on the 8th instant certain papers pertaining to the case of the Canal and Banking Company vs. the United States, with the promise that they would be returned in a few days. This promise has not been fulfilled, and this manner of obtaining papers of the Land Office, not new to you, we consider surreptitious. You will therefore return these papers to this office without delay.

"Yours, etc.,

"HARRY LOTT, *Register.*

"JULIAN NEVILLE, *Receiver.*"

My present letter will be handed to you by my son and partner, Albert C. Janin, who will also exhibit to you the original letter of the Register and Receiver, that the handwriting of Julian Neville may be recognized by any gentleman in the Department. But I have requested my son not to file it, but to return it to me. I want the people here and in Washington City to know what they have to expect when forced to transact business in this Land Office.

After that letter I must avoid all intercourse with the writers thereof that is not imperatively required by professional engagements, and as the law under which this claim of the Canal Bank is prosecuted gives the claimant the choice of going before the Register or Receiver or before the United States Courts, I arrest the proceedings before the former and shall immediately bring suit in the United States District Court in this city.

As further regards that letter, I have of course not answered it, except by informing its writers that I was going to send it to the Department, and that I would request you to direct them to send to the Clerk of the United States District Court, in this city, all documents which have been filed by the Canal Bank as evidence of the claim here spoken of, which are not already in my possession. Requesting to be informed of the result of this application,

I have the honor to be,

Your obedient servant,

LOUIS JANIN.

N. B. The gentleman who has copied my letter just directs my attention to the circumstance that the letter of the Register and Receiver is dated the 17th of January. But I am certain it was written on the 17th of this month. The claim of the Canal Bank was filed on the 16th of last July.

LOUIS JANIN.

On the 30th of September Commissioner Drummond was informed by Louis Janin & Sons, through the undersigned, in a letter of which no copy was kept because it was an informal communication and intended simply as a warning to him, that they had reason to suspect that certain officials in Louisiana were attempting to make use of his office for the perpetration of frauds upon the rights of citizens of New Orleans and Carrollton, and that they hoped he would lend them his assistance in exposing and defeating these frauds.

Below is the Commissioner's answer to this friendly communication. It ought, however, to be stated that during the forenoon of the day on which the Commissioner dictated this letter to his private Secretary, he was closeted for some time with a certain gentleman from Louisiana who is perfectly familiar with the subject. And the undersigned feels justified in stating that their conversation turned upon this very matter, from the fact that on that same forenoon, while he was at the Land Office making inquiries about a copy of Sulakowski's survey which he had ordered, a command came from the Commissioner that it should be given to the gentleman in question.

ALBERT C. JANIN.

DEPARTMENT OF THE INTERIOR, GENERAL LAND OFFICE,

WASHINGTON, D. C., October 2d, 1873.

LOUIS JANIN & SONS,

Washington City, D. C.:

GENTLEMEN—In answer to your letter of the 30th ultimo, in which you announce the discovery of astounding frauds and corruption in what is known as the Sulakowski survey of the townships in which New Orleans and Carrollton are situated, and in which you are pleased to refer to this office as a medium through which these "astounding frauds" are to be perpetrated, I have the honor to state that the lands reported by the Surveyor General as swamp, have not been approved to the State of Louisiana, and that no fraud can be consummated until that is done, as any sale made by the State prior to such approval will become null and void if the swamp claim is rejected. Had this office waited, however, until your recent discovery of these "astounding frauds," before taking measures to inform itself as to the character of the lands and the situation of affairs, I fear that the interests of the people of New Orleans, for whom you express so much solicitude, would have suffered seriously. But you will see, by reference to a copy of a letter to the Register and Receiver at New Orleans, herewith enclosed, that this office ordered an investigation of the matter as early as August 23d, 1773, and caused a notice to be published in English and French, for eight successive weeks, in order that all persons claiming an interest in the lands, or in any wise affected by the claim of the State, under the swamp land grant, might have an opportunity to present their claims at any time prior to December 1st, 1873, and take such steps as they might deem necessary to protect any interest they have in the lands returned as swamp.

The only obstruction that the Land Office at New Orleans has encountered in complying with the instructions of this office, and making the investigations necessary to enable it to protect all legal claims, has been the unwarranted and illegal detention of certain papers borrowed by the senior member of your firm from the local Land Office. As soon as they are returned to the Register and Receiver the investigation will be proceeded with promptly, and all legal rights will be duly respectected and protected.

As the Surveyor General returned and listed the lands as swamp, I am unable to see that the Register and Receiver were guilty of a fraud, or anything wrong in informing the Register of the State Land Office of that fact.

So far as your other charges against United States officials are concerned, I will say that they are too general in their nature to justify this office in making them the subject of investigation; but if you will make them under oath, giving names, dates and particulars, a prompt investigation will be made, and such action taken as the interests of the Government and the public may demand. I regard it as due to the public and to the "theivish officials" charged by you with the grave offence of being implicated in these frauds, and with what you doubtless regard as the still graver offience of making "professions of loyalty and patriotism," that you should make your charges under oath, in a specific form, so that they can have an opportunity of putting in their offence. And I feel very sure, that you, as a gentleman of honor, expressing such deep interest in the public welfare, will not only accord them that privilege, but place the Government in such a possition as to make the proper investigation, and, if need be, rid itself of corrupt and dishonest officials. I earnestly hope that you will make your charges specific, and furnish the proof on which you base them, at the earliest practical moment.

"Very respectfully,

"WILLIS DRUMMOND,

" Commissioner."

WASHINGTON, October 4th, 1873.

HON. WILLIS DRUMMOND :—*(Private.)*

DEAR SIR—We are sorry to find ourselves drawn into an unpleasant controversy with you, not because of any apprehension on our part of injury to ourselves—for we are entirely dependent of any such consideration—but because we desire to practice our profession in peace and without any unnecessary contention and unpleasantness. But you will readily understand that we cannot allow your letter to us of the 2d instant to go unanswered. We therefore ask you to read again our communication of the 30th ultimo, to note how uncalled for the tone and wording your reply are, and to withdraw the latter from your records. If you decline to do this, then we ask, as a matter of right, that our formal answer, herewith enclosed, be also placed upon your records and stand as our reply to your communication of the 2d instant.

Very respectfully yours,

LOUIS JANIN & SONS.

By Albert C. Janin.

DEPARTMENT OF THE INTERIOR, GENERAL LAND OFFICE,
WASHINGTON, D. C, October 15, 1873.

LOUIS JANIN & SONS,
Washington, D. C.:

GENTLEMEN—In reply to your favor of the 4th inst. you are informed that my letter of the 2d inst. was very carefully considered, in fact, every word was dictated by me.

After more mature reflection, I find nothing in it which I desire to withdraw, explain, revise or modify in any respect whatever.

Respectfully,

WILLIS DRUMMOND,

Commissioner.

WASHINGTON, October 4th, 1873.

HON. WILLIS DRUMMOND,
Commissioner of the General Land Office:

SIR—We hasten to acknowledge the receipt of your reply, dated the 2d instant, to our letter of the 30th ultimo, and to express to you the astonishment with which we note the tone and language of your communication. Until better advised, we must indulge the hope that, under the pressure of official business, you signed that letter without a perusal of its contents somewhat more careful and deliberate than is usually required by official communications. It is a matter of painful surprise to us that we cannot call attention, even in an informal way, to the outrageous frauds which certain parties are attempting to perpetrate upon a large body of citizens of New Orleans and Carrollton, without arousing a spirit of hostility and exposing ourselves to personal insults; but that painful surprise is now greatly intensified when we find that, in reply to a friendly letter from us apprising you of the fact (of which you could not be cognizant) that such frauds were being attempted, and that we intended to expose them before Congress, we are assailed in a communicaiion from your office, signed by yourself, in a tone of sarcasm entirely uncalled for, and with charges of matters derogatory to our personal and professional character. If you will carefully peruse our letter to you of the 30th ult., you will see that we made no demand upon your office for an investigation of the matters alleged by us. We stated that we proposed to expose the frauds, denounced by us, at the next session of Congress; we warned you that certain dishonest persons were attempting to make use of your office for their private purposes, and we expressed the hope that, with your assistance, we should succeed in defeating their attempts. We did not look for any reply to this merely informal communication, but if we had, we should have expected a cordial proffer of your aid and support in crushing any attempted fraud upon your office and the rights of private citizens. Instead of this, what do we find? A sneer. We quote from your letter: "Had this office waited, however, until your recent discovery of these 'astounding frauds, before taking measures to inform itself as to the character of the lands and the situation of affairs, I fear that the interests of the people of New Orleans, for whom you express so much solicitude, would have suffered seriously. But you will see by reference to a copy of a letter to the Register and Receiver at New Orleans, herewith enclosed, that this office ordered an investigation of the matter as early as August 23d, 1873, and caused a notice to be published. in English and French, for eight successive weeks, in order that all persons claiming an interest in the lands, or in any wise affected by the claim of the State under the swamp-land grant, might have an opportunity to present their claims at any time prior to December 1st, 1873."

This is nothing new to us, nor, unfortunately, to the people of New Orleans and Carrollton, who are thus put to an immense expense to save their property from spoliation, and made to bear the burden of proof, when the most superficial inspection of most of the land to which we refer, would have satisfied the Surveyor General that he ought not to have approved the survey and listed the lands to the State as swamp lands. But can it be true that the interests of the people of New Orleans would have been seriously endangered if you had delayed such action for one month? Is fraud so swiftly consummated? Before the date of our letter we knew that the survey was all wrong, but we charitably assumed that this was the result of error, and that you would come to the rescue of the parties affected by the error of your subordinates without subjecting them to a ruinous expense to vindicate their rights. Lately, however, we have discovered that this supposed error was the result of fraud, and we so informed you in our letter of the 30th ult., not imagining that you already suspected fraud, since we had not heard of any *investigation* being ordered by you, and were bound to presume that you would have ordered an investigation into the circumstances of the survey and listing of the lands as swamp lands, if you had had any suspicion. We must, therefore, still believe that our information was new to you, and must continue to feel surprised that our promised exposure of the fraud, instead of being welcomed, is sneered at.

So far as that part of your letter is concerned, in which you say that our other charges against United States officials are too general in their nature to justify your office in making them the subject of an investigation, but that if we will make them under oath, giving names, dates and particulars, you will investigate them, we have only to state that we have not asked of your office any such investigation. As we have already informed you, we fully intend to make the promised exposure, "giving names, dates and particulars," at the proper time and place, and if we cannot get from you the co-operation and assistance which we promised ourselves, that fact will only make our task more laborious, though, we confidently hope, none the less successful. The thievish officials whom we charge with fraudulent conduct will be furnished by us with all the opportunity you bespeak for them for vindicating themselves; but we prefer to be ourselves the custodians of our proofs, until the proper time for submitting them arrives. So much for the matters of public concern of which your letter treats.

We now wish to say a few words in relation to personal matters:

1. If you are not too much engrossed with official business, you will much oblige us by favoring us with an explanation of the precise meaning of the latter part of the following sentence which we find in your communication: "I regard it as due to the public and to the thievish officials charged by you with the grave offence of being implicated in these frauds, and with what *you doubtless regard* as the still graver offence of making 'professions of loyalty and patriotism,' that you should," etc., etc. We dislike covert insinuations, and before making any reply to this one, we desire to be clearly informed what is meant by it.

2. You take the responsibility of charging the senior member of our firm with the unwarranted and illegal detention of certain papers borrowed from the Land Office at New Orleans. Perhaps it has not occurred to you that it would be advisable and more consistent with propriety to investigate the matter and ascertain the truth of the charge you thus make, before, upon the authority of an ex-parte statement by letter and telegram, venturing to indorse, in an official communication, the unfounded calumny of a corrupt subordinate. You can, without difficulty, satisfy yourself that the papers you refer to were in reality never *filed* in the Land Office, but were merely left there by the counsel of the Canal Bank to be copied, and were freely and voluntarily given to the senior member of our firm for the purpose of having them translated, and they were never even demanded of him, although he was on several occasions subsequently in said office, until he undertook to thwart the attempts of the Receiver to extort illegal fees from his clients. The papers belong absolutely to the Canal Bank, and are probably filed by this time in the clerk's office of the United States District Court for Louisiana. Nor is it true that the withdrawal of the papers has given rise to any delay in the investigation of the claim of the Canal Bank. Investigate the matter, and you will soon discover how much reliance is to be placed upon any statement emanating from Julian Neville, the Receiver in question.

We remain, etc.,

LOUIS JANIN & SONS.

NEW ORLEANS, *October* 10, 1873.

HON. WILLIS DRUMMOND,

COMMISSIONER OF THE GENERAL LAND OFFICE.

SIR—I received this morning from my sons and partners in Washington City your letter to my firm of the 2d instant, in which, to my great surprise and regret, you charge me with professional delinquency, and treat with derision the sincere expressions of contempt and indignation with which, in private letters to my sons, I spoke of the nefarious frauds with which land owners in the vicinity of this city are now threatened under color of law.

I had no idea that my sons would communicate these opinions to you, as I demanded no action. I am not the knight-errant of justice to everybody, and I have seen many frauds practiced in land matters, in my long career, without interfering when my clients were not directly interested. But my sons, knowing that I am familiar with the subject, and that I do not advance accusations lightly, believed in them, and thought proper to prepare you for the coming disclosures. For I know that they will come, though I, at my advanced age, desire peace, and did not wish to be the spokesman.

My immediate client, the New Orleans Canal and Banking Co., whose property has been sectionized and sold as swamp land subject to tidal overflow, at twenty-five cents an acre, including the canal, the shell-road, the half-way house, the hotel at the lake end, the Metairie race course, and a cemetery, for all of which the bank is responsible as warrantor, has no interest in the swamp land question. For that corporation has a complete final grant from the French Government of Louisiana, of the 6th of October, 1757, of record in the original book of French concessions—such a title as should have been confirmed without special application, under the Act of 1805. But as you challenged me, without any proposition of my firm, to proffer charges, I shall do so, if you deem it to the public interest, and shall do so over my name and under oath, and substantiate the charges by evidence, although I shall receive no compensation for this disagreeable trouble and loss of time. My motive is to show that the sympathy which I privately expressed for this, in land matters, very much oppressed community, was sincere, and not, as would appear from the tone of your letter, ridiculous affectation. A passage in your letter warrants the remark that I do not intend, for the first time in my life, to be drawn into a political controversy. I speak of the proprietary interest in land matters only. All that I claim is that my strictly professional communications may be treated by the present head of the Land Department with the same courtesy which they received from his numerous predecessors during the many years that I had business before them.

But what concerns me personally is to repel the charge of professsonal misconduct which you make upon the statement of Mr. Julian Neville, the Receiver of the Land Office. I can ascribe this only to yonr want of attention to the letter I addressed to you on the 18th ult., or to your not having received it. In July last, the New Orleans Canal and Banking Company filed in the New Orleans Land Office a claim for the confirmation of a tract of land represented on Sulakowski's survey of T. 12, S., R. 11 East., S. E. District of Louisiana. Messrs. Lea, Finney & Miller, the counsel of the Bank, filed a notice, and also deposited a number of documents to be used as evidence in the case; one an original, the others certified copies obtained from various offices. In September last, Messrs. Lea, Finney & Miller, requested the Bank to employ me in that case, as I was more familiar with the local titles than they were. I looked at the papers, found them numerous, mostly in foreign languages, which required translation for use of the Government employees, and, in fact, such papers as could not be satisfactorily studied in such an office. I therefore requested Mr. Harry Lott, the Register, to let me take them home to study them and have them translated. This request was very courteously granted by Mr. Lott. I, of course promised to return them as soon as possible, or whenever they were wanted, though nothing was said of the precise time of returning them, as I could not determine what time the translators would require.

Previously, Mr. Stoek, of the firm of Hosmer & Co., had written to the Register and Receiver that his firm had been employed by the State of Louisiana to examine the claim of the Canal Bank, and asked for the appointment of a day for a conference. The Register and Receiver appointed the 11th of September, and Mr. Stoek, by letter, promised to attend. On that day I was in the Land Office, and Mr. Lott asked, "where are the papers?" and I answered, "there," pointing to a black satchel, in which the persons in the Land Office have constantly seen me carrying my papers. As I am very friendly with Mr. Stoek, I requested the Register and Receiver and their clerk to send him, if he arrived, right to my lodgings, where the documents were being translated, and where I could have given some explanations that would have saved him a good deal of trouble. But on the 11th of September we did not suppose that he would come, as the yellow fever was then reported to be prevalent, and the conference was adjourned to the first of October. And nobody asking to look at the papers, I left them in my satchel, and took them home, my translator not having yet finished his work.

These translations were finished on the 17th ultimo, and on the 18th I received by mail the following astonishing letter:

New Orleans, January 17, 1873.
(Ought to have been September.

"Louis Janin, *Attorney at Law, No. 79 Bienville street.*

"Sir—You obtained from this office, on the 8th inst., certain papers per-"taining to the case of the Canal and Banking Company vs. the United "States, with the promise that they would be returned in a few days. This "promise has not been fulfilled, and this manner of obtaining papers from "the Land Office, not new to you, we consider surreptitious.

"You will, therefore, return those papers to this office without delay.

"Yours, etc.'

"HARRY LOTT, *Register,*
"JULIAN NEVILLE, *Receiver.*"

This letter of Mr. Neville, whom you call a bonded officer of the United States, was a deliberate and intentional insult to me. Why he singled me out for his impertinence, what his disgraceful motives were, will become apparent to you during the sequel of his official career.

I transmitted a copy of that letter to you in a letter of the 18th of last month, and stated to you that, after having been thus addressed, I could have no further intercourse with those persons, and was going to transfer the prosecution of the claim from the New Orleans Land Office to the District Court of the United States in this city, under the provisions of the Act of Congress, of June 22, 1860, revived by the Act of Congress of June 10, 1872, which gives this choice of jurisdiction to claimants. I do not believe that any lawyer with self-respect could have acted differently.

I never received an answer from you to that letter, but I informed the Register and Receiver of its contents, without, however, indulging in recrimination or discussion, and then I received the following letter, dated the 24th of September, signed by Julian Neville alone:

"LOUIS JANIN,

"*Attorney at Law, Bienville street,*

"Your note of 23d instant, is at hand, and I have to say that it is not sat-"isfactory.

"You obtained papers from this office in a manner very disreputable. We "have demanded their return, and you reply that you have taken the case "from this office. We do not know you in the case. You promised to return "the papers on the 9th inst. Have you done so? No. You took advantage "of a trust placed in you and retained the papers—this is your usual game.

"You say you have filed the papers in the District Court. This is not true "—another attempt at deception. You say you have written to the Com-"missioner at Washington. We are glad to hear it. We have also written "to him; and in our letter we told him of the appreciation you had of him—"of the gross language you expressed towards him, both in this office and "that of the Surveyor.

"We have seen the District Attorney, who agrees with us as to your ob-"taining the papers. If they are not returned we will take measures to ob-"tain possession.

"JULIAN NEVILLE,
"*Receiver.*"

Of course I did not answer that letter. With his usual veracity, Mr. Neville advanced that I had said that I had filed the papers in Court, whereas, after having received the first insolent letter of the 17th ultimo, I simply wrote to the office, without recrimination or abuse, that I had retained the papers, and that I would retain them since they were the property of my clients, and the land office had no further use for them, as I had concluded to transfer the case to the United States District Court.

This transfer, however, required the preparation and copying of a petition. I was in no particular hurry, since I had determined not to continue the case in the land office, nor to give Mr. Neville an opportunity to annoy my clients by refusing to give up the papers, and compelling them to take out fresh copies

On the 27th of September the Cashier of the Canal Bank received the following letter:

CHARLES JUMONVILLE, ESQ.,
Cashier Canal and Banking Company.

DEAR SIR—We are instructed by telegraph from the Commissioner of the General Land Office, received this morning, to refuse Mr. Janin any access to the records of this office, and not to recognize him as an attorney. We shall obey instructions, and place the whole matter in the hands of the United States District Attorney.

Very respectfully, your obedient servants,

HARRY LOTT, *Register.*
JULIAN NEVILLE, *Receiver.*

My petition having been finished and copied, I filed it in the United States District Court, together with every one of the papers I had obtained from the land office.

In the meantime my letter to you of the 18th ultimo, above mentioned, remained unanswered. Even in your letter of the 2d inst., addressed by you to our firm in answer to a letter written to you by its members in Washington, on the 30th ult., you do not allude to it. Did you never receive it? If so, I can account for your belief in Mr. Neville's assertions.

The very morning of the 18th ult., when I received the first insulting letter, I went to the land office and asked Mr. Tully, the clerk, whether all the papers I had withdrawn had been copied. He answered in the affirmative. Mr. Neville sat within a few feet of the clerk, but I did not speak to him, nor he to me.

I submit that it has been the invariable practice of the land offices in Louisiana, when its members were sitting as boards of commissioners, to return the evidence to the claimants after it had been examined and filed. What immense danger claimants would run if their titles could be taken from them is best illustrated by the present condition of these land offices! In this case, the evidence had heen copied into records of the land office. What business could that office have with the original copies, since the case was withdrawn from it and preparing for the District Court?

Mr. Neville's object was blackmailing, of which infirmity he has given other instances.

As your letter of the 2d inst., to my firm by its tone imposes upon me the obligation of proffering charges, I shall do so, as my more serious business may give me time to do it, and I shall begin with Mr. Neville. I am ready to make a charge against him of so distinct a character that it can be understood at once without a complicated enquiry. But it requires the copying of voluminous papers, and may not be ready before a certain number of days.

I have the honor to be, sir, your obedient servant,

LOUIS JANIN.

DEPARTMENT OF THE INTERIOR, GENERAL LAND OFFICE,

WASHINGTON, D. C., Oct. 15th, 1873.

MESSRS. LOUIS JANIN & SONS,

Attorneys at Law,

Washington, D. C.:

GENTLEMEN—By a letter dated September 20th, 1873, the Register and Receiver of the U. S. Consolidated Land Office at New Orleans, Louisiana, informed this office that on the 8th of that month the Senior member of your firm, Louis Janin, Esq., "by false representations and promises," borrowed from that office, and refused to return, the papers filed and of record in the case of the N. O. Canal and Banking Co. vs. the U. S., then pending before said Register and Receiver, under the act of June 22d, 1860, (12 Stat. p. 85) and supplemental legislation. In reply this office, having directed those officers to again make a demand for the return of said papers and report the result, and having been notified by them that demand had been made and that the said papers had not been returned to their custody, addressed a telegram and a letter both dated September 26th, 1873, to the said Register and Receiver, directing them neither to recognize Mr. Louis Janin as attorney nor permit him to have access to the records and papers of their office.

Since this action I have received a letter dated Oct. 10th, 1873, from Mr. Louis Janin, by which it appears that said papers have not been returned but have been filed in the U. S. District Court of Louisiana, from which it clearly appears that it is not the intention of your firm to again place said papers in the office of the U. S. Register and Receiver at New Orleans. I have, therefore, by telegram of this date, directed the U. S. Surveyor General for Louisiana, until further orders, to deny the firm of Louis Janin and Sons access to his records and papers, except for the purpose of preparing charges against Government officials, and to refuse to recognize them as attorneys before his office under any circumstances; and by letter of this date I have communicated similar instructions to the Register and Receiver of the U. S. Land Office at New Orleans.

In view of your continued refusal to return the records borrowed as aforesaid of the local Land Office at New Orleans, it becomes my duty, as an officer, to take such measures as may be necessary to protect the Government and parties having business before this office and subordinate offices from a further interference with public records by parties who have wantonly violated the confidence reposed in them, and disregarded well established rules of professional propriety and practice, and I have, therefore, now to inform you that from and after this date, and until further notice from the Commissioner of this office, you will not be permitted to examine any record or paper filed herein, unless such examination be for the purpose of obtaining data in support of any charges you may desire to make against officers of the Government, nor from this date, until such notice, will you be recognized as attorneys in any case now pending or which may hereafter be presented to the General Land Office.

Very respectfully,

"WILLIS DRUMMOND,

" *Commissioner.*"

POSTSCRIPT.

As the unjustifiable attack of Commissioner Drummond upon myself and my law firm, and our professional character and business, has placed me in the somewhat ridiculous attitude of a martyr sueing for justice. I can assure the numerous persons for whom we have business necessarily coming before the General Land Office, and among others our distant client the City of Baltimore (under John McDonogh's munificent bequest), that, conscious of the entire rectitude of my professional course throughout a long life, and fully acquainted with the rights of my profession and of the citizens I represent, and having also resided at Washington City for a considerable number of years, I am too well informed of the enlightened fairness of Mr. Secretary Delano and of the disposition of Committees of Congress to act fairly, at least where no political questions are involved, to entertain the least apprehension for our clients' interests from the Commissioner's hostility to me and my firm. And the many citizens of New Orleans, whose property-rights are directly threatened by the fraudulent entries of land based upon Sulakowski's and Ross' survey, may rest assured that the opposition which we have encountered from Commissioner Drummond and his subordinates in this city will neither deter us from exposing the frauds in question, nor prevent us from being entirely successful in defeating the dishonest schemes of the speculators engaged in them.

LOUIS JANIN.

New Orleans, November 4th, 1873.

www.ingramcontent.com/pod-product-compliance
Lightning Source LLC
LaVergne TN
LVHW011140110826
845150LV00008B/2429
* 9 7 8 1 4 1 8 1 9 3 4 2 3 *